Guggenheim

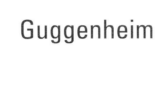

Editorial coordination and text:
Aurora Cuito

Appendix text:
Pablo Soto

Graphic Design:
Mireia Casanovas Soley

Layout:
Emma Termes Parera

Translation:
Michael Bunn

Copyediting:
Bill Bain

Photography:
© Eugeni Pons
© Pepe Ruz: Pages 185, 186 and 187
© Pep Escoda: Pages 188-201
© Bill Timmerman: Page 203, © Friederich Busam: Page 205, © Hisao Suzuki: Page 207
© Jean Marie Monthiers: Page 208, © Hickey + Robertson: Page 209, © Lock Images: Page 211
©Ana Quesada: Page 212, © Robert Canfield: Page 213, © Lidia Rodríguez: Page 214-215

© Worldwide edition: Kliczkowski Publisher - Asppan S.L.
La Fundición, 15. Polígono Industrial Santa Ana
Rivas Vaciamadrid. 28529 Madrid. Spain
Tel.: +34 91 666 50 01
Fax: +34 91 301 26 83
e-mail:asppan@asppan.com
www.onlybook.com

ISBN: 84-89439-53-2
D.L: B-21.106/2001

Editorial project

LOFT Publications
Domènec 9, 2-2
08012 Barcelona. Spain
Tel.: +34 93 218 30 99
Fax: +34 93 237 00 60
e-mail: loft@loftpublications.com
www.loftpublications.com

Printed by:
Apipe Artes Gráficas, Sabadell. Spain

May 2001

Guggenheim

Foreword

Bilbao invents its future

Bilbao is concentrated almost in its entirety along the meandering final stretches of the River Nervión, a ria, or drowned river estuary. The stretch the city occupies is a hollow surrounded by mountains which form a natural barrier, giving rise to the traditional name of the city: *botxo*, which means "hole" in the Basque language.

Bilbao was originally a fishing village on the banks of the ria, a key geographic feature in that it gave the city its raison d'être and its importance. The ria has always been an excellent communication route between the sea and the inland area, and is navigable along most of its length. At present, commercial navigation – which still reaches as far up as the University of Deusto – is on the point of disappearing from the interior of the city. The numerous projects and urban planning alterations are progressively changing the physiognomy of the banks of the Nervión.

Industrial development, which grew from the profits made from the iron market, created wealth and employment for almost a century. In 1985, however, the city experienced a profound economic crisis which led to the advent of post-industrialism – the manufacturing worker ceased to be a central supporting figure for industry, and the new urban classes, connected with communications, culture and leisure, built on the ruins of the old shipyards.

At the beginning of the nineties Bilbao bounced back, and in a surprising manner: it was decided that a social change was needed, and this would begin with the construction of a museum. Close collaboration between the Basque authorities and the Guggenheim Foundation led to the creation of a new museum which would represent the current spirit of the city.

This building, designed by Frank O. Gehry, was not the only change, however: Norman Foster designed the plans for the renovation of Bilbao Metro, and there was the Zubizuri bridge, the Santiago Calatrava airport terminal, the Palace of Congress and the Palace of Music (by Soriano and Palacios) as well as the urban planning reorganisation carried out by César Pelli.

All of these projects offer a new image of the city which attracts tourism, creates business opportunities and employment and which has, in short, turned Bilbao into one of the most emblematic cities in Europe, one which has a very bright future ahead of it.

Guggenheim International

New York **Solomon R. Guggenheim Museum** **Guggenheim Soho** **Project for new Guggenheim Museum** Venice **Collection Peggy Guggenheim** Bilbao **Museo Guggenheim** Berlin **Deutsche Guggenheim**

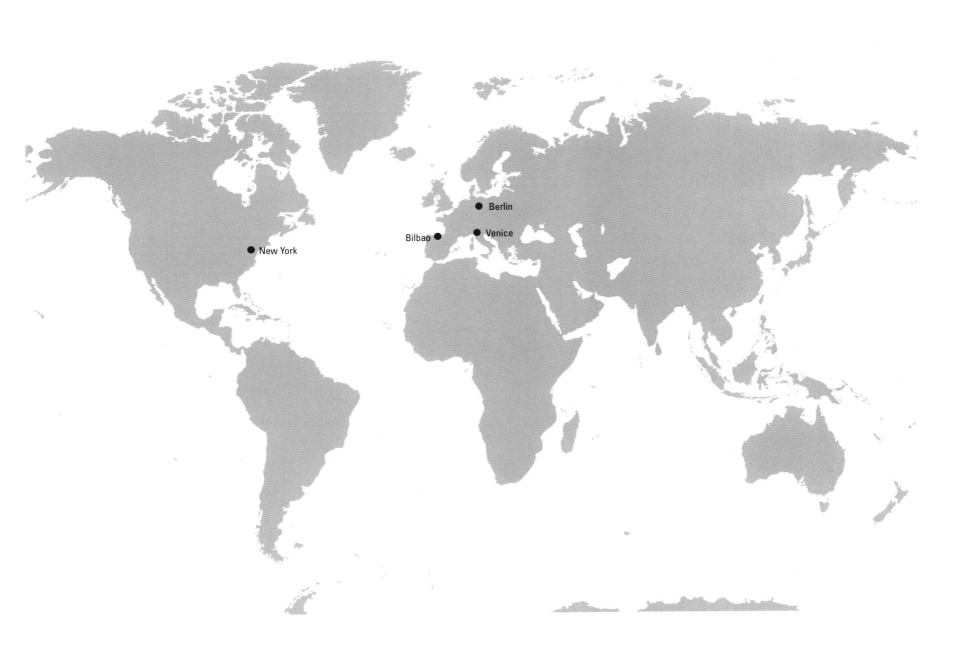

New York's Solomon R. Guggenheim Museum

"We need a fighter, a lover of space, an agitator, an inventor and a wise man...I want a temple of the spirit, a monument." Hilla Rebay to Frank Lloyd Wright, 1943.

In June 1943, Frank Lloyd Wright received a letter from Hilla Rebay, art consultant to Solomon R. Guggenheim. Rebay was asking Wright to design a new building to house the Guggenheim Museum for abstract painting. Owing to the innovative lines of the design, the project turned into a battle between the architect and his clients, the local functionaries, the art world and public opinion. Although Wright and Guggenheim both died before building work was finished in 1959, the museum had become proof of Wright's architectural genius and the adventurous, audacious personality of its founder.

Wright did not hide his disappointment at Guggenheim's decision to locate the museum in New York.

"I've thought of lots of other places in the world to build this museum in," he said, "But we'll have to try this city." New York for him was overpopulated, too built-up and lacking in architectural interest. But after considering different locations, the museum was located on Fifth Avenue, between 88th Street and 89th Street, next to Central Park, so that nature would absorb some of the noise and congestion of the city.

And that natural space, which offered a break from the urban bustle, also inspired the form of the building; in fact, the spiral design is reminiscent of a shell, with continuous spaces which flow in and out of each other.

Wright installed lifts to take visitors up to the top of the building, from where they could descend by a series of ramps which took them past the works of art. The galleries are compartmentalised like the membranes in citrus fruit: independent but all interconnected. The central empty space around which the ramp gyrates allows the visitor to enjoy, simultaneously, art pieces located on different floors.

Some people – above all, artists – criticised Wright for creating a museum which subjugated the art it contained.

"On the contrary," wrote Wright, "I designed the space to generate a continuous harmony between the building and the paintings." Wright dreamed up a magnificent building full of organic and geometric references; architecture which continues to appear just as original and refreshing as it was 40 years ago.

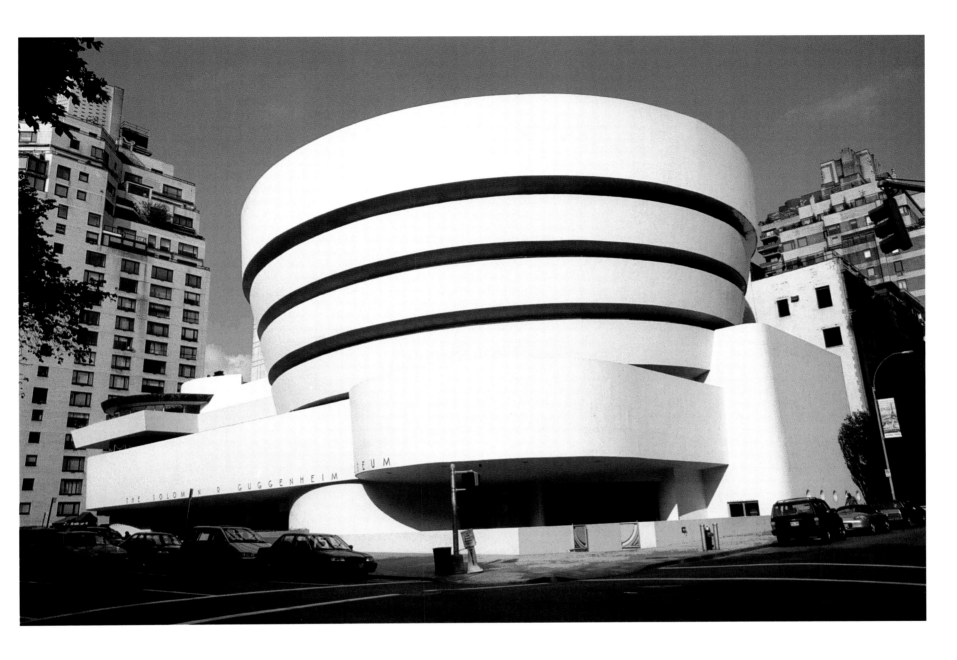

Frank Lloyd Wright

Frank Lloyd Wright (1869-1959) was born in Richland Center, Wisconsin. After dropping out of high school in 1885 he started working as a draughtsman and attended courses in civil engineering at the University of Wisconsin. In 1887 he moved to Chicago and began work at the studio of Dankmar Adler and Louis Sullivan. The latter influenced him to such a degree that Wright referred to him as Lieber Meister. In 1893, Wright opened his own office.

The houses he built in Buffalo and Chicago won international renown in those areas where avant-garde movements had become popular, especially in those countries in which industrialisation had created conflict in terms of architecture and urban planning. In the United States, his clients were small, go-ahead institutions and businessmen who were individualistic, practical and independent.

He combined commissions for country houses with others for commercial buildings, churches, schools and even a museum: the controversial project for the Solomon R. Guggenheim museum in New York, which provoked criticism and passionate defence in equal parts. The design sacrifices part of the building's functionality in order to create a new way of looking at works of art, especially in those points from which galleries on other floors can be seen.

Wright's death in 1959 robbed the world of an architect who dared to imagine what was fascinating instead of conforming to what was probable.

Solomon R. Guggenheim

Solomon R. Guggenheim (1861-1949) was born in Philadelphia, and was the oldest son of Meyer Guggenheim, a Swiss immigrant who had amassed a considerable fortune from importing and marketing products from the land of his birth.

After a sound education at Swiss and American schools, Solomon began working in his father's company. Later, with his six brothers, he founded the company Guggenheim Brothers. During the 1920s, by which time he had retired, he began collecting works of art, and by the age of 65 he owned several works from the Italian Renaissance, but knew almost nothing about paintings. After meeting Hilla Rebay, a young German woman, he changed his ideas about the plastic arts, and especially about experimental tendencies in contemporary European painting. Tempted by the idea of becoming a pioneer in a specific area of art collection, Guggenheim started the first-ever Kandinsky collection in the world. In 1937 he established the foundation that bears his name, and in 1939 he officially opened the Museum of Abstract Painting in New York. Since 1959, his entire collection has been on show in the Solomon R. Guggenheim Museum, another building designed by Frank Lloyd Wright.

The Peggy Guggenheim Collection in Venice

The Peggy Guggenheim Collection, one of the most prestigious modern art museums in Europe, bears the name of the famous heiress who founded it. Guggenheim built this collection up herself in London, Paris and New York between 1938 and 1947. It includes representative works from artistic movements such as cubism, surrealism and American abstract expressionism.

In 1948 Peggy Guggenheim put on an exhibition for the first time in Europe, during the Venice Biennial, a year later she buying the Veneir dei Leoni Palace, a sumptuous unfinished building on the Grand Canal of Venice. The palace later was, opened to the public as a museum and she donated to the Solomon R. Guggenheim Foundation.

The Foundation took on the responsibility of ensuring the museum's future and carried out a series of improvements.

The space encircling the building was transformed into a sculpture garden, opened to the public in 1995. The collection includes sculptures from the collections of Raymond and Patsy Nasher and of Peggy Guggenheim herself. The enlargements to the museum, carried out between 1993 and 1995, were designed by the architect Clement de Thiene, and include a shop, a restaurant, halls for temporary exhibitions and the expansion of the garden. The interiors were designed by the New York firm Vignelli Associates.

In 1995, the exhibition spaces of the garden pavilion were restored and furnished with donations from prestigious companies such as Knoll and Arclinea. The new wing and the recent work carried out in different parts of the palace have made it possible for the entire Peggy Guggenheim collection to be housed under the same roof

Peggy Guggenheim

Peggy Guggenheim (1898-1979), the niece of Solomon R. Guggenheim, was born in New York. In 1912, her father and her brother perished in the sinking of the Titanic. She inherited the family fortune on reaching her majority in 1919. Unhappy with her commodious bourgeois life, a year later she married Lawrence Vail and the two adopted a Bohemian life style. When the marriage failed, she moved to Paris and opened a gallery to exhibit and sell modern art.

In 1941, she returned to New York and married the surrealist painter Max Ernst, but two years later they divorced. She inaugurated another gallery and became the patron of many young artists, among them Jackson Pollock, Mark Rothko, and Robert Motherwell.

Soho Guggenheim Museum

In recent years, the exhibitions organised by the Guggenheim Foundation have occupied the halls of more than 80 museums around the world. As a result of this growth, the organisation has tripled the number of people visiting its exhibitions, and has been forced to enlarge the exhibition space. The Soho Guggenheim Museum opened to the public in 1992. It is located in Soho, a district which is distinguished by its wrought iron and brick constructions. The remodelling of the existing building was carried out by one of the winners of the Pritzer architecture prize, the Japanese architect Arata Isozaki. The museum's large rooms contain a permanent collection of post-Second World War works and temporary exhibitions. Among the artists featured in recent retrospective exhibitions are Robert Rauchenberg and Andy Warhol.

Arata Isozaki

Arata Isozaki (Oita, 1931) studied architecture in Tokyo and began working as a professional architect under the tutelage of Kenzo Tange. Considered to be one of the most important Japanese architects of the generation which followed that of his master, Isozaki's work represents an indisputable point of reference for younger architects. During the nineteen-sixties he participated in the Metabolistic movement, which proposed the creation of large urban infrastructures to which other buildings could be added, in a process of continuous transformation. Noteworthy buildings of his from this period include the Oita Central Library (1964-1966), the Middle Level School in the same city (1964) and, above all, the plan conceived together with Tange and Kurokawa for the urban development of Tokyo (1960).

His later works, however, were not subjected to such strict theoretical laws. Isozaki has become an intellectual architect who bases his projects on a conscientous study of the cultural environment which is to frame his constructions. Thus, his work becomes an architectural interpretation of his particular view of each place.

Deutsche Guggenheim of Berlín

The Deutsche Guggenheim in Berlin is located in the renovated old centre of the city. The name of the museum derives from those of its creators, the Deutsche Bank and the Solomon R. Guggenheim Foundation, an alliance which represents a novel collaboration between a banking organisation and a museum. Both share responsibility for the exhibition programs and the administration of the museum.

This museum represents a special connection with the historical roots of the Guggenheim family, which originally came from Germany. At present, the Guggenheim Foundation owns a significant number of German art works and regularly organises exhibitions for German artists.

The building's halls are home to between two and three large exhibitions a year, most of which are retrospectives of a particular artist.

The Deutsche Guggenheim of Berlin is situated in one of the head offices of Deutsche Bank, which is a stone building constructed in 1920. The American architect Richard Gluckman fitted out the interior, a space which is governed by simplicity and purity of forms. A staircase was installed which joins up the exhibition halls with the shop and the café, from where the visitor can enjoy a view of the covered patio space.

Plans for the new Guggenheim Museum in New York

The Guggenheim Foundation has commissioned the architect Frank O. Gehry with the project of designing a new museum, which will be located in south Manhattan, on the East River. The construction will stand on six large pillars that will be anchored directly onto the rocky bed of the river. A flat platform installed at street level will be the base for the museum, and there will be a square which will contain various public installations, including a car park and a skating rink which in summer will become a garden.

There will be a large glazed atrium situated in the centre of the square which will contain the information area, the museum entrance and a café. From this central space visitors will pass on up to a second level that leads to the exhibition areas which, as a result of their elevated position, will have a magnificent view of the river.

This new Guggenheim complex will be comprised of five elements: the permanent collection, the temporary collections, the centre of art and technology, the centre of architecture and design and a tower which will contain some of the museum's service areas, as well as a restaurant and a small hotel.

Standing like a sculpture on the banks of the river, the new Guggenheim will make the south of Manhattan into a unique cultural centre.

The Guggenheim in Bilbao

The Guggenheim Museum in Bilbao

The Guggenheim Museum in Bilbao, Spain, is the result of close collaboration between the Government of the Basque Country (which financed the project and is its owner) and the Solomon R. Guggenheim Foundation, which organises the museum and supplies it with art works.

The museum represents the first step in the resurgence of what used to be an old commercial and industrial area located on the banks of the River Nervión. Easily accessible from the financial district and the old city centre, the museum stands in the centre of a triangle formed by the University, the City Hall and the Museum of Fine Arts. A public square situated at the entrance of the complex encourages pedestrian traffic between this building and the Museum of Fine Arts, and between the old city centre and the river. The La Salve bridge, which connects the urban centre to the outlying districts, crosses the east side of the site and gives the museum the distinction of acting as an entrance gate into the city.

The museum's main entrance takes the form of an enormous central atrium, from where a system of curvilinear bridges, glazed lifts and different stairways provide communication between the three floors of the exhibition galleries in a concentric fashion. A sculptural ceiling rises from the central entrance hall and serves to fill the space with light that enters through enormous glazed apertures. The unprecedented dimensions of the atrium – which reaches a height of fifty metres above the level of the river – serves to attract visitors into the complex.

The Guggenheim Foundation commissioned various spaces – spaces which would contain a permanent collection, temporary exhibitions and a selection of works by living artists. To satisfy these requirements, three types of halls were designed: the permanent collection can be seen in two sections of three adjoining square spaces, which are located on the second and third levels of the museum. The temporary exhibitions are on show in an elongated rectangular gallery which extends eastwards, stretching out beneath La Salve bridge to finish in a tower. The selection of works by living artists is on show in a series of curvilinear galleries which are scattered throughout the museum and which allow the visitor to view these creations in relation to the other two collections.

The predominant materials for the exterior of the building are limestone and titanium panels, used for the rectangular forms and for the sculptural curves, respectively. An enormous curtain wall provides magnificent views of the river and of the city.

The design of the museum is clearly influenced by the scale and textures of the city of Bilbao; it evokes the materials that were used in the old industrial buildings at the river's edge, and shows a deep respect for the historical, economic and cultural traditions of the area.

Project Leaders

Client: Solomon R. Guggenheim Foundation /Bilbao Guggenheim Museum Foundation

Architects: Frank O. Gehry & Associates, Inc.
Head of design: Frank O. Gehry
Head of project: Randy Jefferson
Project coordinator: Vano Haritunians
Project architect: Douglas Hanson
Project designer: Edwin Chan
Team: Bob Hale, Rich Barret, Karl Blette, Tomaso Bradshaw, Matt Fineout, David Hardie, Michael Hootman, Grzegorg Kosmal, Naomi Langer, Mehran Mashayekh, Chris Mercier, Brent Miller, David Reddy, Marc Salette, Bruce Shephard, Rick Smith, Eva Sobesky, Derek Soltes, Todd Spiegel, Jeff Wauer, Kristin Woehl.

Architects and associated engineers: IDOM (Bilbao, Spain)
Project manager: José María Asumendi
Project coordinator: Luís Rodriguez Llopis
Project architect: César Caicoya
Team: Jorge Garay, Javier Ruiz de Prada, Javier Mendieta, Antón Amann, Cruz Lacoma, Amando Castroviejo, José Manuel Uribarri, Rogelio Díez, Ina Moliero, Fernando Pérez Fraile, Pedro Mendarozketa, Miguel Rodriguez, David Prósper, Javier Aróstegui, Víctor Zorriqueta, Juan José Bermejo, Fernando Sánchez, Javier Aja, Juan Jesús García, Álvaro Rey, Armando Bilbao, GonzalO Ahumada, Javier Dávila, Imanol Mújica, Rafael Pérez Borao, Juncal Aldamicechevarría.

Consultants:
Architectural consultant: Carlos Iturriaga
Representatives of the Solomon R. Guggenheim Foundation: Thomas Hut, Andy Klemmer.
Structural engineering: Skidmore, Owings & Merrill (Chicago, USA)
Mechanical engineering: Cosentini Associates (New York, USA)
Lighting: Lam Partners (Boston, USA)
Acoustics and audiovisuals: McKay, Connant, Brook, Inc. (Los Angeles, USA)
Theatre: Peter George Associates (New York, USA)
Security: Roberto Bergamo E.A (Italy)
Curtain wall: Peter Muller, Inc (Houston, USA)
Lifts: Hesselberg Keese & Associates (Mission Viejo, USA)

Builders:
Foundations: Cimentaciones Abando
Steel and cement: Ferrovial / Lauki / Urssa
Exterior: Construcciones y Promociones Balzola
Interiors, construction systems and building work: Ferrovial

Surfaces:
Site: 32,700m^2
Building: 28,000 m^2
Galleries: 10,560 m^2
Public space: 2,500 m^2
Library: 200 m^2
Auditorium: 605 m^2
Offices: 1,200 m^2
Shop: 375 m^2
Restaurant: 460 m^2
Café: 150 m^2

Frank O. Gehry

Frank O. Gehry grew up in Toronto, Canada, and moved to Los Angeles with his family in 1947. He studied architecture at the University of Southern California, graduating in 1954. He then continued his studies at the Harvard University Graduate School of Design. After working with the architects Victor Gruen and Pereira & Luckman in Los Angeles, and with André Remondet in Paris, France, he set up the firm Frank O. Gehry Associates Inc. in 1962. Since then, Gehry has pursued a solid professional career which has spanned four decades, designing public and private buildings in America, Europe and Asia.

Pieces of note designed by Gehry include (in the nineteen-sixties) a line of cardboard chairs and a hay barn in San Juan de Capistrano, USA (1968). The seventies saw the studio for Ron Davis (1972), the Gunther, Familian and Wagner line of houses which were never built, and his own residence, which introduces materials considered of little value to architecture.

In the eighties, Gehry designed the space for an exhibition in Los Angeles on Russian constructivism. His architecture them took a radical turn toward complex structures made up of simple volumes. This was the approach used for the California Aerospace Museum (1984) the Loyola School of Law (1984) the Winton and Schnabel residences, all located in the USA. In 1989 he was awarded the prestigious Pritzker architecture prize, the first recognition he had received in his career, although he has since never ceased to receive recognition.

During the nineties, his simple volumes were transformed, his spaces became warped and less geometric and more organic. This is the case with the Guggenheim Museum in Bilbao and National Nederlanden's head office in Prague.

There is not one single Gehry, there are several of them. There is the Gehry who carried out experiments on the perception of objects in perspective and the use of cheap, undervalued materials in architecture, such as wire mesh and cardboard, then there is the Gehry who introduced figurative elements into architecture and who changed the scale of the commonest objects, the Gehry who adopted the compositional strategies of the Russian constructivists by arranging systems based on simple pieces, and the Gehry who created buildings comprised of sinuous membranes, thanks to a little help from NASA computer programs.

There is a clear difference between the experimental exercises of his early days and the important role that the media has played in the popularity of his current buildings. It could be said that as a consequence Gehry has discovered his own ability to surprise others, and clients from all over the planet flock to his office to ask for and a show.

◁ **T**he museum stands on the banks of the River Nervión, next to a much-traversed hanging bridge which, from the very start, Gehry conceived as an intrinsic part of the project. The staircases and lifts which take the visitors from the raised bridge down to the level on which the museum stands are encased by a vertical steel and stone construction.

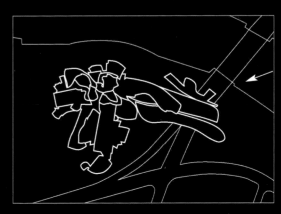

◄— The arrow shows the point from which the photograph was taken.

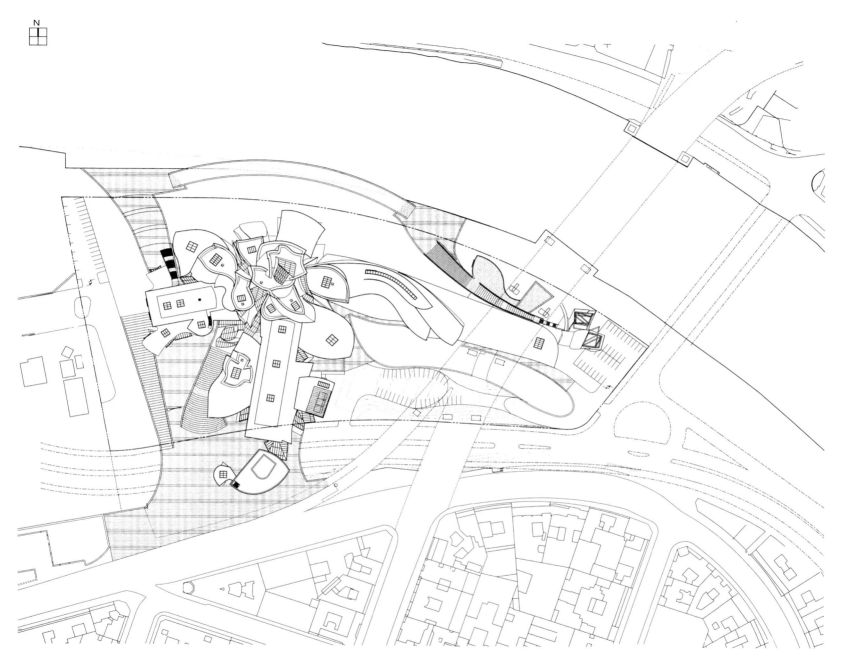

Location plan

scale: 1/2500

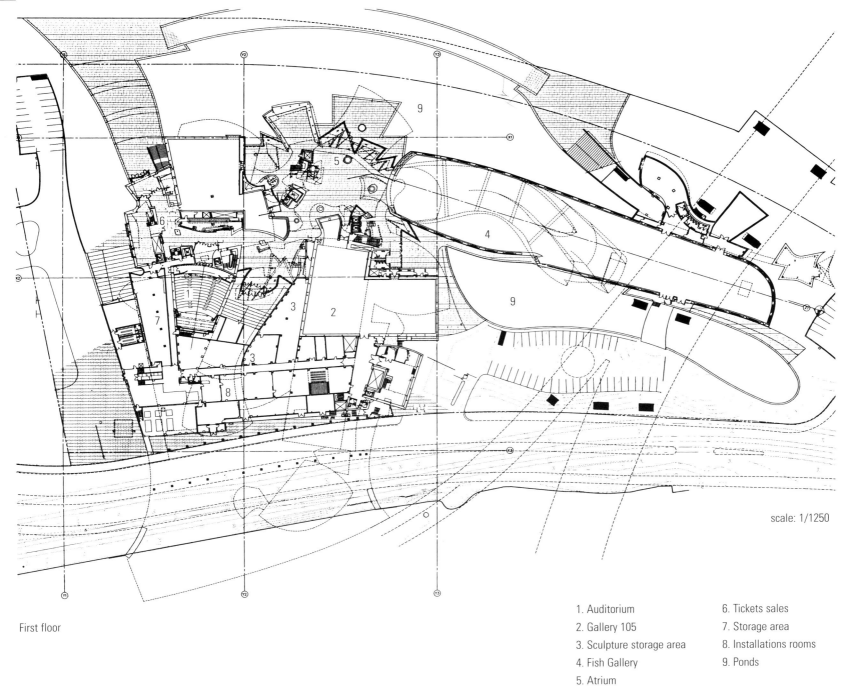

9

5

6

4

1

7

3

2

3

9

8

scale: 1/1250

First floor

1. Auditorium
2. Gallery 105
3. Sculpture storage area
4. Fish Gallery
5. Atrium

6. Tickets sales
7. Storage area
8. Installations rooms
9. Ponds

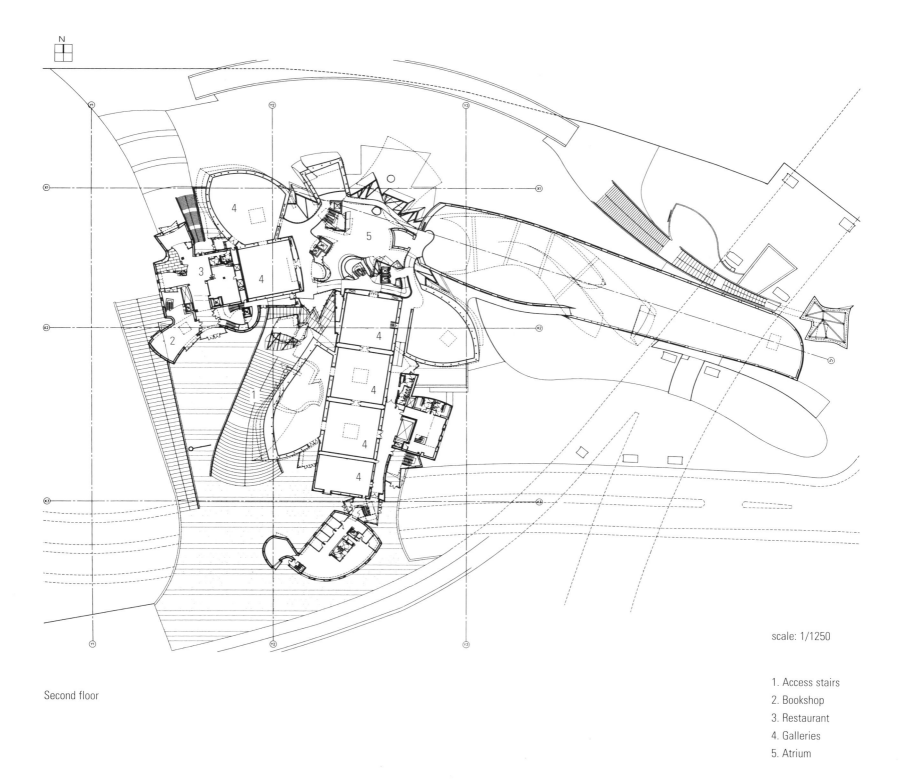

N

Second floor

scale: 1/1250

1. Access stairs
2. Bookshop
3. Restaurant
4. Galleries
5. Atrium

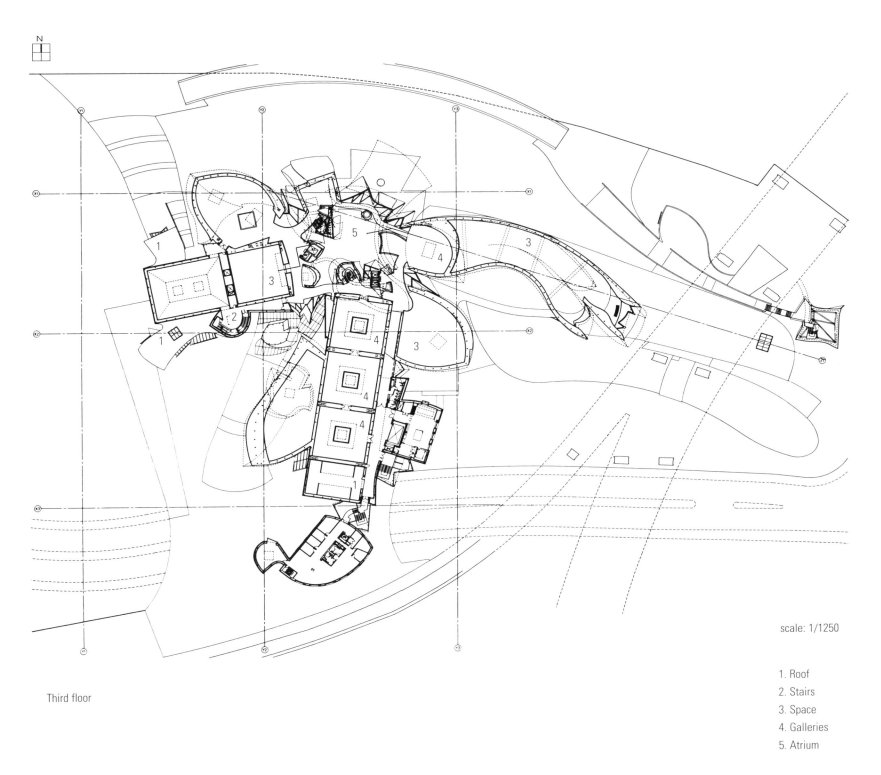

N

scale: 1/1250

Third floor

1. Roof
2. Stairs
3. Space
4. Galleries
5. Atrium

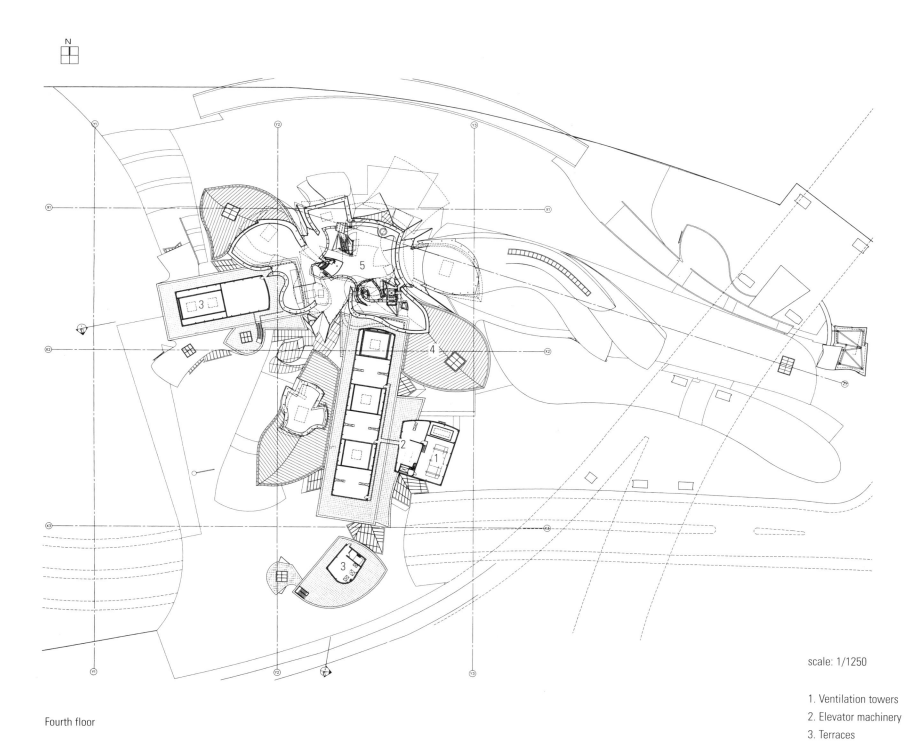

N

scale: 1/1250

Fourth floor

1. Ventilation towers
2. Elevator machinery
3. Terraces
4. Roofs
5. Atrium

N

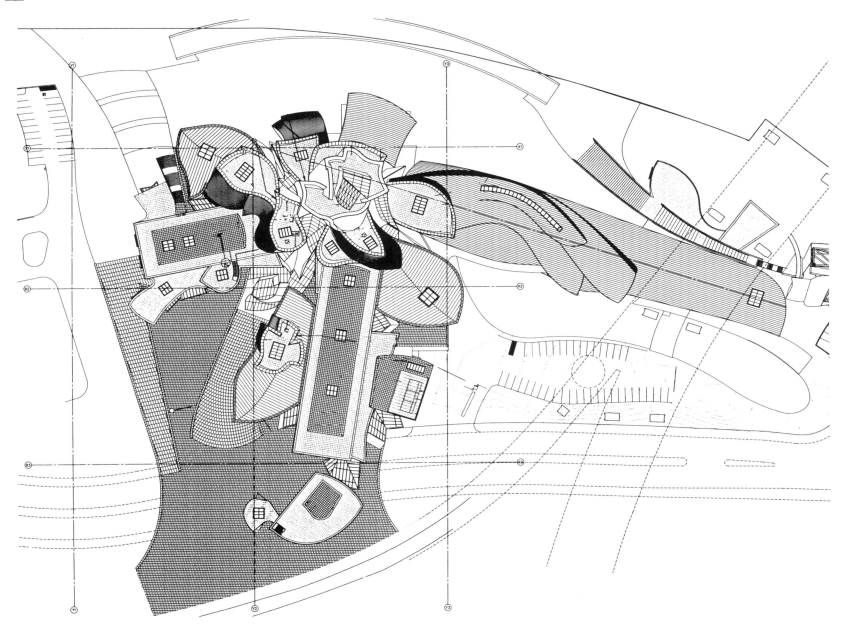

Roofs

scale: 1/1250

◁ **B**oth the Basque authorities and the representatives of the Guggenheim Foundation were looking for a singular, iconoclastic building which on one hand would repeat the impact created by the construction of the New York Guggenheim by Frank Lloyd Wright, and on the other, which would serve as an advertisement that would attract the gaze of the cultural world and establish the city on an international level.

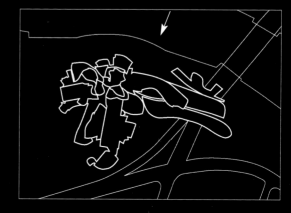

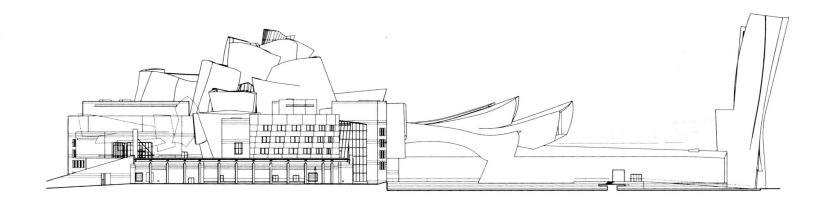

South elevation

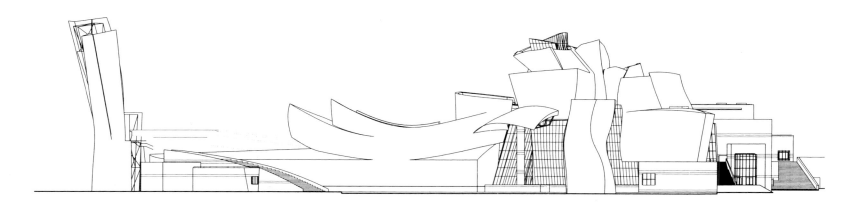

North elevation

scale: 1/1000

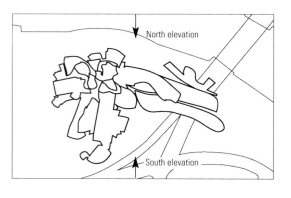

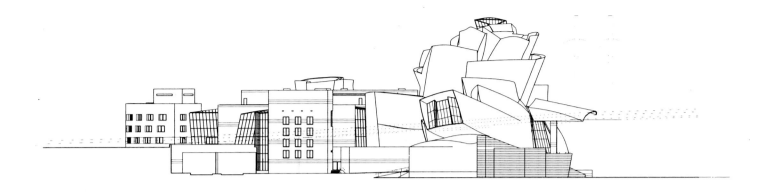

East elevation

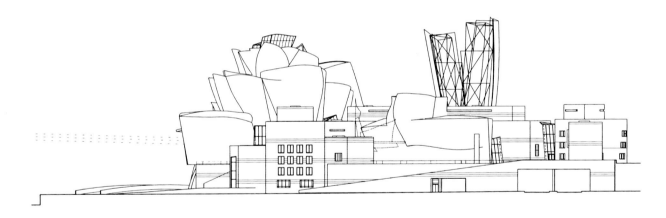

West elevation

scale: 1/1000

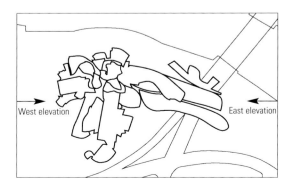

West elevation   East elevation

The building's unusual form invites many comparisons and similes, however, the references used for the design were Fritz Lang's Metropolis, Brancusi's sculptures and, above all, the very energy and contained strength that is radiated by the city of Bilbao.

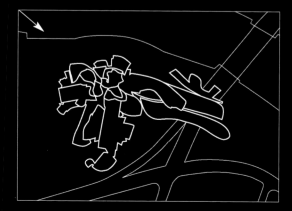

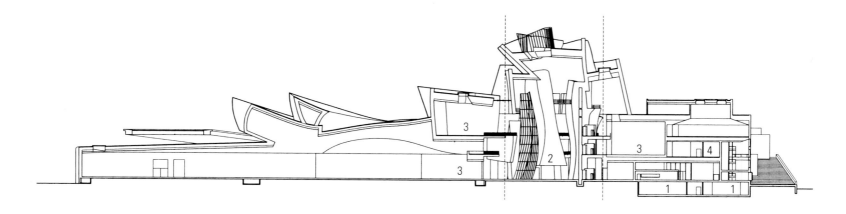

Section A-A'

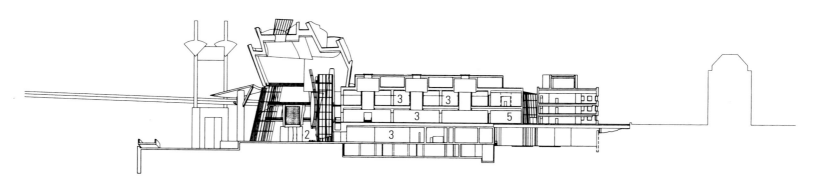

Section B-B'

scale: 1/1000

1. Storage area
2. Atrium
3. Galleries
4. Kitchen
5. Bookshop

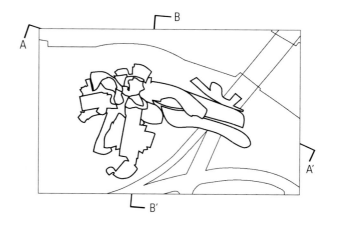

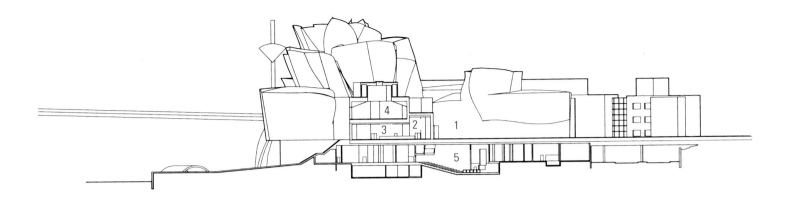

Section C-C'

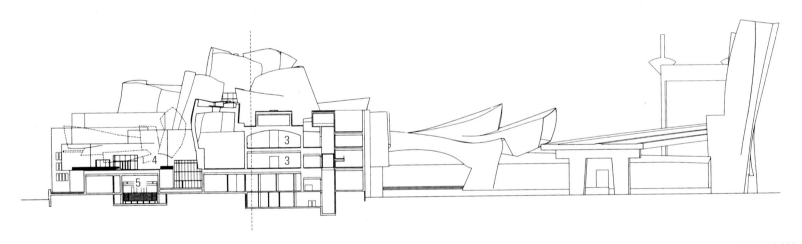

Section D-D'

scale: 1/1000

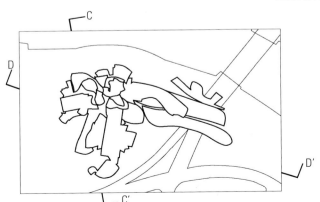

1. Plaza
2. Café bar
3. Galleries
4. Restaurant
5. Auditorium

Details

The building's curved volumes have been covered with titanium, a metal which is ductile, flexible, elastic and hard-wear- ▷ ing. The museum is the first large construction to have been finished in this material, following an exhaustive research process. Titanium was chosen for its striking appearance and its high resistance to pollution and the effects of the weather.

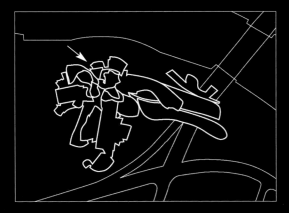

At the Gehry studio they have a rather unusual way of working: the plans are ▷
developed by means of multiple sketches and models made out of different materials
which are then transferred – almost literally – to the computer screen, where they are
analysed mathematically in order to work out technical and structural points.

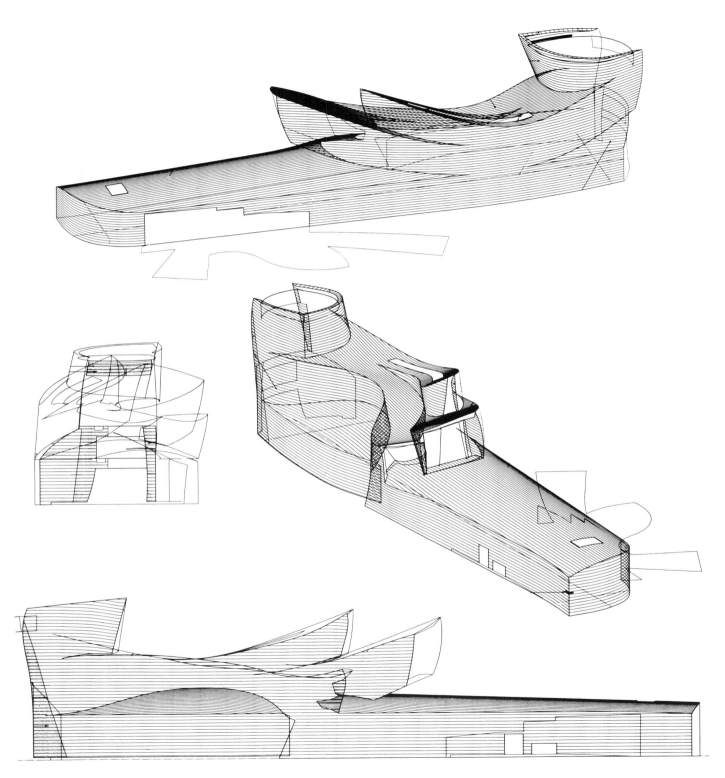

Developmental perspective of the titanium skin

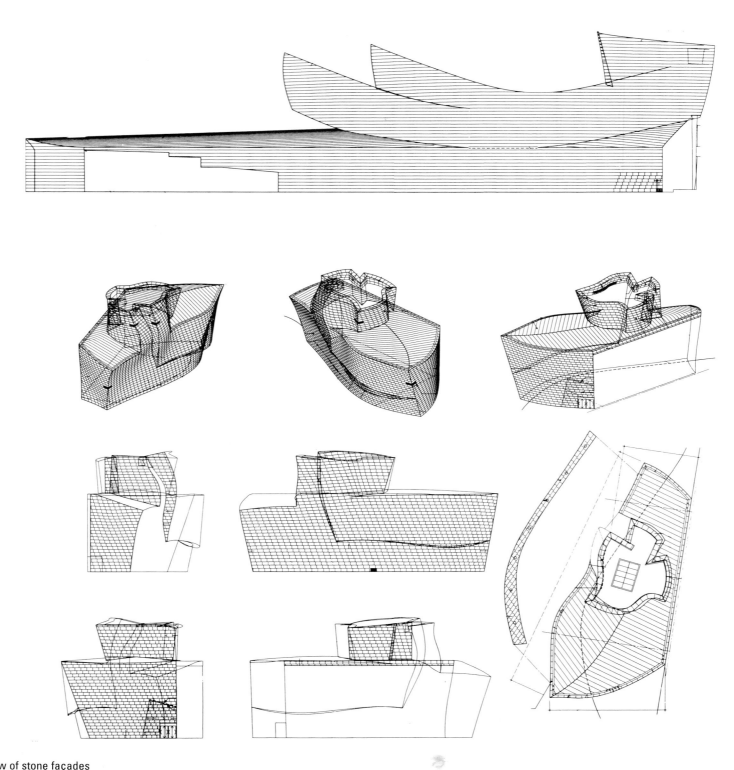

Schematic view of stone façades

◁ **S**ince the titanium sheets are very thin (only 0.3 mm), strong winds cause them to warp slightly, though this does not represent a structural problem. To create the enclosures, 60 tons of titanium was used, which was made into 33,000 "scales" by means of a special lamination process.

◁ **O**ne of the pecualiarities of titanium is its versatility: the high degree to which it reflects the light produces multiple effects from the different facades. Thus, with the first rays of the sun, the museum looks as if it has been silver-plated; by midday its effect is almost blinding, while as the sun sets it takes on a golden colour.

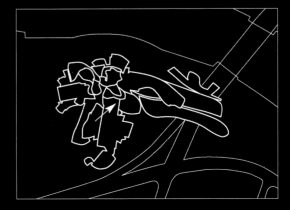

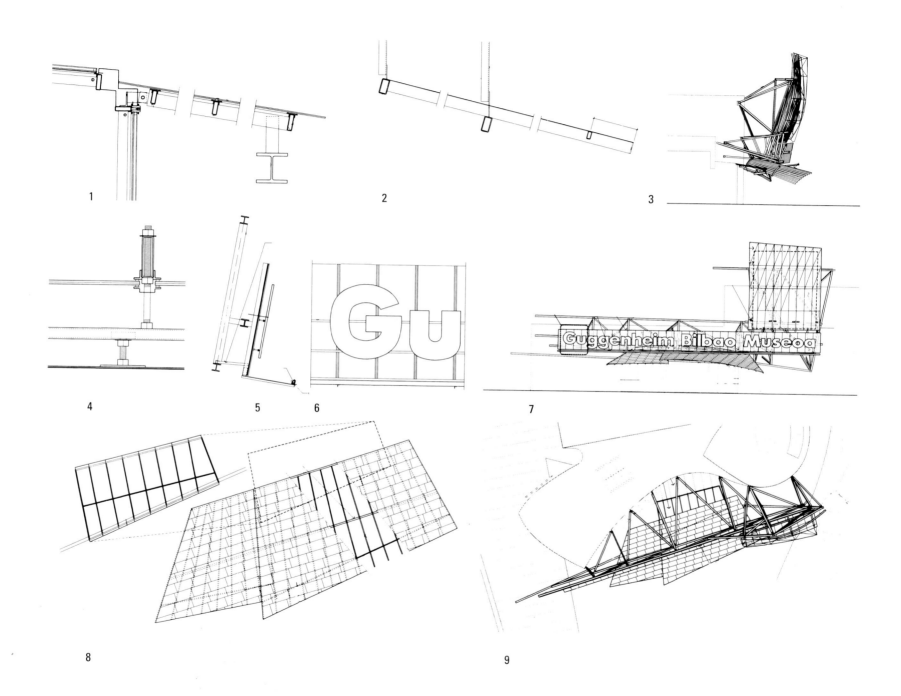

1

2

3

4

5

6

7

8

9

◁ **T**hese diagrams show the construction details of the entrance and the sign bearing the name
1. Section of the glazed roof
2. Section of the metal roof
3. General section
4. Detail showing the anchoring of the upper letters on the sign
5. Section of the sign
6. Elevation of the sign
7. General elevation of the sign
8. Plan of the glass and metal roofs
9. Plan of the roof at the entrance

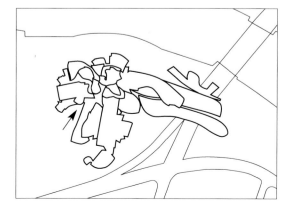

Interiors

Temporary exhibitions

May 98-June 98	Form and imagination: masterpieces from the Blake-Purnell collection	Rooms 302 and 303
June 98-October 98	After mountains and sea: Frankenthaler 1956-1959	Room 103
July 98-October 98	China: 5,000 years	Second and third floor
November 98-February 99	Cristina Iglesias	Room 103
November 98-March 99	Robert Rauschenberg: retrospective	Rooms 104, 301, 302, 303 and 304 , second floor
March 99-May 99	From Durero to Rauschenberg	Rooms 305, 306 and 307
March 99-October 99	Richard Serra	Room 104
April 99-September 99	Chillida: 1948-1998	Second floor
October 99-January 00	Andy Warchol: a Factory	Second floor
November 99-September 00	Motorcycle art	Room 104
January 00-May 00	David Salle	Rooms 103 and 105
February 00-May 00	The tower struck by lightning: the impossible as a goal	Rooms 301, 302, 303 and 304
February 00-June 00	Clemente	Second floor
June 00-September 00	From Degas to Picasso: painters, sculptors and the camera	Rooms 301, 304, 305, 306 and 307
June 00-August 00	Amazons of the avant-garde	Room 103
October 00-February 01	Perceptions in transformation: the Panza collection from the Guggenheim Museum	First, second and third floors

Museum collection

October 97-June 98	The Guggenheim museums and the art of the 20th century	All the museum
April 98-December 99	Recent European art	Room 105
November 98-February 99	The avant-garde and expressionism in the 20th century	Rooms 305, 306 and 307
March 99-December 99	American pop art	Room 103
March 99-July 99	Contemporary Basque and Spanish art	Rooms 301, 302, 303 and 304
May 99-May 00	Modern painting and sculpture	Rooms 305, 306 and 307
July 99-January 00	International trends in contemporary art	Rooms 301, 302, 303 and 304
July 99-December 99	Contemporary photography: in-depth views	Room 105
June 00-September 00	American pop art	Room 103
June 00-September 00	Sugimoto: portraits	Room 303
June 00-October 00	The European avant-garde	Room 202
June 00-October 00	Works on paper	Room 204
June 00-October 00	American and European postwar art	Rooms 203, 205 and 206
June 00-October 00	The resurgence of painting: the nineteen-eighties	Room 207
June 00-October 00	Richard Long	Room 208
July 00-October 00	Anselm Kiefer	Room 209

◁ **T**he art works have to be carefully illuminated, a point which led to in in-depth study being carried out on the light available in the exhibition halls. Natural light never directly influences objects, it creates a warm, continuous atmosphere in which the focuses of light uncover specific details.

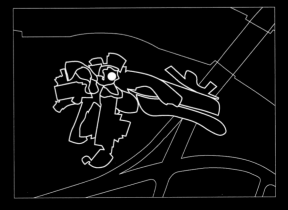

Frank O. Gehry was unable to resist the temptation to give expression to one of his obsessions – the form of a ▷
fish – in one of his masterworks. The largest hall in the building, colloquially known as the "Fish gallery",
extends beneath the La Salve Bridge, creating a space 130m long and 24m high; this space is used for exhibiting examples of pop art, minimalism and conceptual art produced by American artists since the sixties.

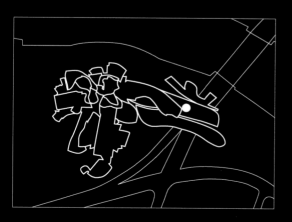

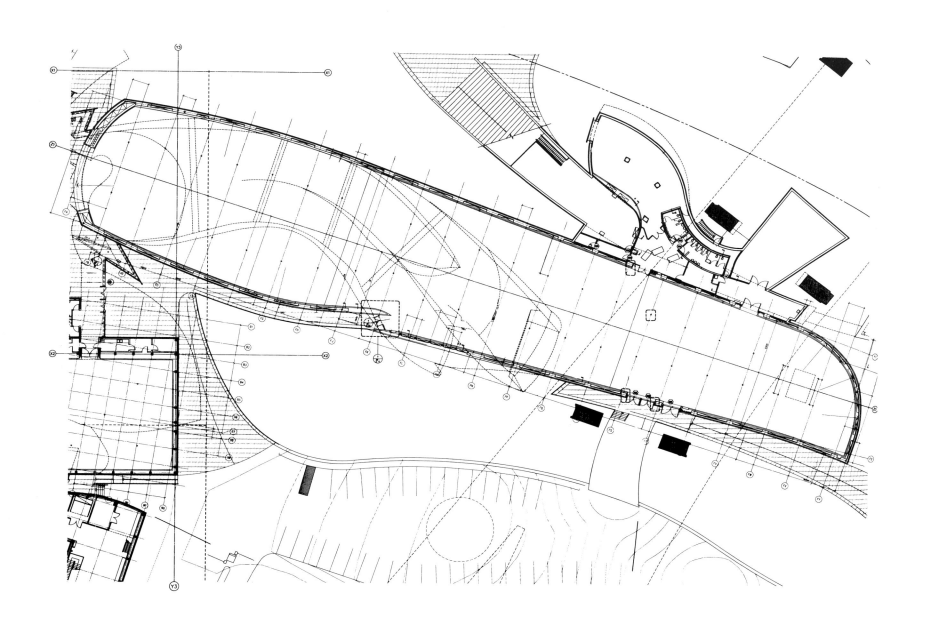

Plan of gallery 104

◁ **T**he library contains a wide selection of art books within a space divided into different levels. These halls were also designed by the Frank O. Gehry studio, and represent an attempt to create an ambience that blends in with the perceptive sensations of the exhibition areas.

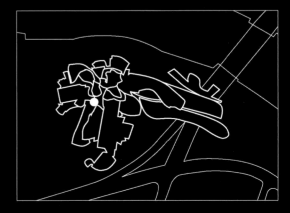

EARTH TO E
ASHES TO A
DUST TO DU

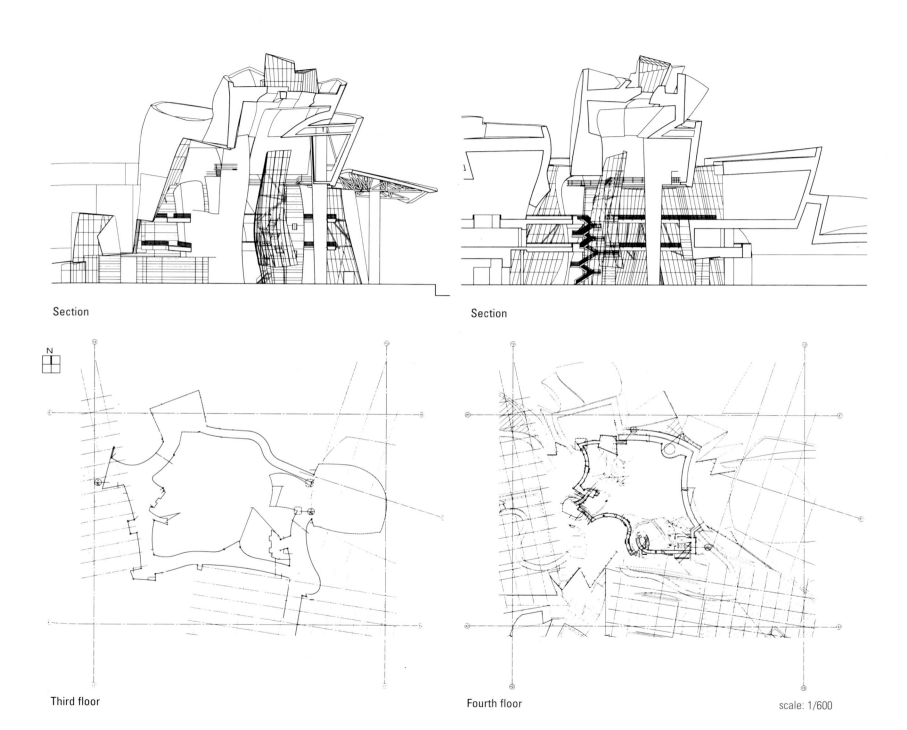

Section

Section

N

Third floor

Fourth floor

scale: 1/600

Sections and plans of the central atrium.

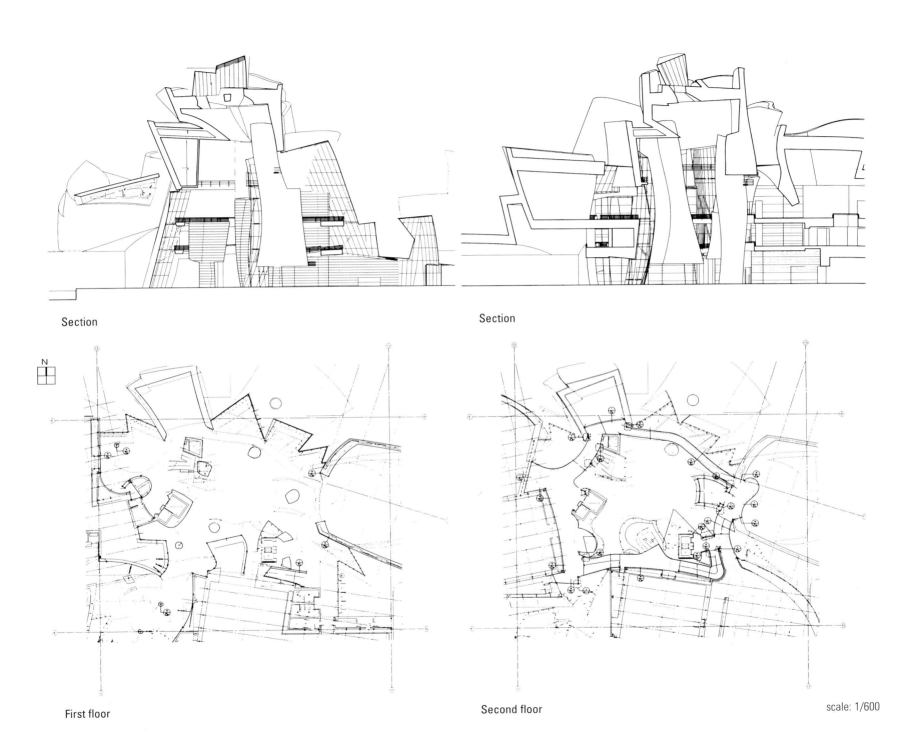

Section

Section

N

First floor

Second floor

scale: 1/600

Sections and plans of the central atrium.

◁ **T**he museum is articulated around a large central atrium 50m in height (one-and-a-half times the height of the entrance hall of the New York Guggenheim) and which is crowned by a metal flower and illuminated by means of a large glazed section that also has a metal structure. The central space organises the flow of visitors and sends them off into the three different exhibition areas.

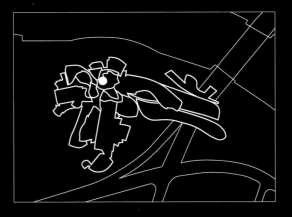

The museum's functionality, as well as its structure, is governed by common sense. It has been designed with ▷ consideration not only for the comfort of the visitors, but also with a view to the maintenance of the complex. A good example of this is the location of the hanging bridges in the central atrium, which provide access to the interior of the façade so that the glazed sections can be cleaned more easily.

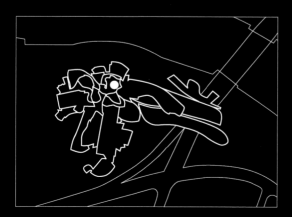

The New Bilbao

Ría de Bilbao

Alameda de Recalde

Ercilla

López   de   Haro

Diego

Elcano

Plaza
Moyua

Don

Elcano

Vía

Alameda de Recalde

Gran

Ercilla

Plaza de
Arriquibar

Plaza de
Zabalburu

Indautxu

Autonomía

Autonomía

Autonomía

Barriada Urizar

Casco Viejo

E

Public institutions

1. Provincial government
2. City council
3. Town hall

Points of interest

1. San Mamés Field
2. Vista Alegre Bullring
3. Post Office
4. Trade Fair
5. Bilbao Stock Market
6. University of Deusto
7. Plaza Nueva
8. Alhóndiga
9. Doña Casilda Park
10. Begoña Basilica
11. Municipal Market
12. Arriaga Theater
13. Chamber of Commerce
14. Ayala Theater
15. Coliseo Albia Theater

Museums

1. Museum of Fine Art
2. Museum of Artistic Reproductions

3. Basque Archeological, Ethnographic, and Historical Museum
4. Guggenheim Museum

Transport Stations

1. Abando Station (Renfe)
2. Atxuri Station (Eusko Tren)
3. Naja Station (Renfe)
4. Concordia Station (FEVE)
5. Casco Viejo-Zazpi Kaleak Station (Eusko Tren)

Bridges

1. Deusto Bridge
2. Salve Bridge
3. Zubizuri Bridge
4. Town Hall Bridge
5. Arenal Bridge
6. Merced Bridge
7. Ribera Bridge
8. San Antón Bridge

Metro Stations

◁ **T**he industrial reconversion of Bilbao has led to the the abandoning of many already-obsolete manufacturing installations. As a consequence, a few years ago the local authorities developed a policy of regeneration for the area along the river. One of the actions included in the policy was to build more bridges over the River Nervión, thereby creating a greater connection between the two riverbanks. The most emblematic of these bridges is the one designed by Santiago Calatrava, and which has become one of the symbols of the new Bilbao.

Bilbao is a city with a long tradition of metallurgy and iron and steel industries. The River Nervión, which ▷
divides the city into two, has always been the central focus for the iron and steel industry, shipyards,
enormous cranes and warehouses, which for many years have shaped the image of the city. A hard landscape, but at the same time one which possessed great strength, and in which the new buildings have
been located, such as the Palace of Congress, designed by the architects Soriano and Palacios.

◁ **N**orman Foster approached the construction of Bilbao metro on the premise of employing specific qualities that would identify the city. Overriding any formal decision in Foster's architecture is the possibility of improving the quality of life of the city's inhabitants. This is achieved on the basis of a more human and friendly architecture that gives priority to street lighting and correct functional organization.

The technical solutions adopted by Santiago Calatrava for his buildings might be extremely sophisticated, but they give the appearance of naturalness: hence their proximity to nature, to animal skeletons and to trees. With the new terminal for Sondika airport, for example, the construction has the appearance of a large shell which opens minimally to give access to the users of the building.

A walk through Bilbao

◁ During the eighties, Bilbao was plunged into a profound industrial crisis which left in its wake a desolate panorama of pollution and degradation. During the latter years of the twentieth century, the disappearance of the dilapidated factories was followed by the cleaning up of the ria itself, resulting in an environmental regeneration that has turned the city into a place which is cleaner, more cheerful and with a better quality of life.

Como tu cielo es el de mi alma triste

y en él llueve tristeza a fino orvallo,

y como tú entre férreas montañas,

sueño agitándome.

Miguel de Unamuno

Like your sky is my sad soul / and in it the sad rain falls finely, / and, like you, between iron mountains, / I agitatedly dream.

Bilbao's gastronomic tradtion is one which is deeply rooted in popular culture. ▷
The excellent fresh produce available from the sea, together with the culinary imagination of
the people of Bilbao, has produced such delicious local dishes as *kokotxas* and Bilbao-style cod.

Vives en mí, Bilbao de mis sueños,

sufres en mí, mi villa tormentosa,

tu me hiciste en tu fragua de dolores

y de ansias ávidas.

Miguel de Unamuno

You live in me, Bilbao of my dreams, / you suffer in me, my stormy town / that fashioned me, in its forge of pain / and thunderous anxiety.

◁ **T**he structures which Santiago Calatrava designs are not conceived as simple zoomorphic analogies; it is the end result that evokes nature: "My work is more figurative than organic, in the sense that what interests me are certain anatomical-sculptural associations. Working with isostatic structures inevitably leads back to the patterns that are visible in nature."

Through the Eye of the Lens

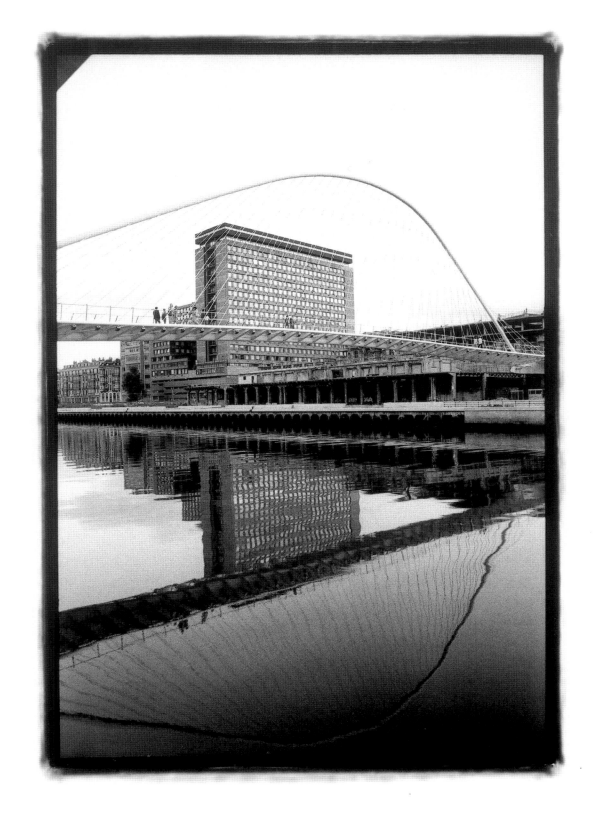

Appendix

Popularity, proliferation and change
in the contemporary exhibition space

The recent advent of buildings such as the Bilbao Guggenheim Museum by Frank O. Gehry (1997), the extension of the Jewish Museum in Berlin by Daniel Libeskind (1998), and the recently-finished Tate Modern in London by Herzog & De Meuron (2000) make it necessary for us to reflect on present-day museological practice. The great popularity and proliferation of cultural and exhibitory spaces experienced at the end of the twentieth century seem to be unequivocal signs of the validity and growth in importance of the contemporary museum, in both strictly architectural terms as wel as in commercial and ideological ones. Currently, no city that wishes to make its mark on the international map nor any architect who belongs to the elite of this discipline can avoid the challenge and need to create an emblematic building which is dedicated exclusively to cultural promotion and the exhibition of art. Nowadays, museums represent not only a singular building within the urban fabric, but also exist as their own kind of distinguishing mark both of the architect that designed them and of the city to which they belong.

The path that led to the democratising of the museum space is approximately 500 years old. The first collections of art were private ones which appeared with the Italian Renaissance, and thus a differentiation was created between Renaissance-style decoration and collections of ancient art works. During the century of the Enlightenment, the next step towards the concept of the museum consisted of the divulgation of the private collections of noblemen and women, who felt that their subjects should also be allowed to see their works of art. In spite of the advances made in the mentality of society during that age, the commissioning of architectural projects specifically to build museums was still not very common. It was not until the French Revolution that the National Assembly decreed that a museum should be created in the Louvre galleries. This pioneering spirit, which was oriented towards developing museums that would be open to the general public, reappeared two centuries later when President Georges Pompidou opened a competition to design a cultural centre for Paris "which will at the same time be a museum and a creative space."

Without ceasing to exist as mediator par excellence between artistic production and the spectator, the contemporary museum maintains the original spirit of the French example. However, the traditional function of the classical museum as a didactic instrument (which, as we mentioned previously, only began to appear as a

public, organised institution at the beginning of the twentieth century) is increasingly giving way to a more playful conception of approaching art. This attitude is clearly represented in the planning of these projects which, apart from the traditional areas of exhibition, storage and restoration, more and more frequently incorporate leisure-oriented sections such as restaurants, bookshops and multi-purpose halls which may be used for anything from book launches to shows of different kinds. It was the Georges Pompidou Centre (Renzo Piano & Richard Rogers, Paris 1977) that first sparked a great rapprochement between the public and such a traditional institution as a museum; since that particular example of "Hi-tech machinery" appeared in the interior of the traditional Beaubourg area of Paris, a great deal of controversy has been created regarding this kind of cultural installation, both in the press and on television, with opinions ranging from the harshest criticism to the wildest acclamation.

This controversy continues to resound, and serves not only to provoke further comments from the press and the public, but also constitutes the kernel of all contemporary museum-based production; it seems that even now definitive parameters have still not been established for the purposes of commissioning an architectural project for a museum. The only point that seems to be clear is that they should be turned into leisure spaces. The traditional relationship between the work of architecture, the work exhibited and the spectator, ranges from positions which opt for a daring design capable of turning the museum into both a work of art and a self-publicising construction, to those that prefer a discreet space which can contain, without distractions, the works of art upon which the visitor's attention should be centred. Whatever the criteria chosen, the museum should aspire to be an ambience of mediation, and a place for the art work and the public to meet; the latter should be given clear, direct information on what is on show, and all of this within a pleasant atmosphere. The validity of the museum as an institution is rooted both in the degree to which society needs it and in the topicality of the a for mentioned controversy, which is generally protagonised by governments, exhibition curators, museum directors and, very occasionally, by the art works or their creators.

In just the last 30 years, 600 museums have been constructed in the United States, and a similar proliferation has taken place in Europe. The increase in demand for, and production of this kind of building derives from the public's growing interest in art as a new kind of spectacle, as well as from the fact that there are now more cultural policies which aim to satisfy this need by the public authorities and private institutions, and thirdly, from the current abundance of contemporary art styles and diversity of format, which would be difficult to show in a traditional exhibition space. It is

possible, for example, to imagine Picasso's "Guernika" in a location other than the room in the Reina Sofia Museum in Madrid which was especially designed for the painting, or Richard Serra's "The Snake" in a location different to the Boat Gallery in the Bilbao Guggenheim, or Louis Bourgeois' "Maman" in the interior of the large central turbine hall in the Tate Modern in London. Increasing artistic production demands new places to exhibit it in which, apart from being merely exhibition sites, also become centres for cultural promotion, with added commercial and tourist attractions.

Currently it is not unusual to find museums designed to contain private art collections or works of specific artists, as for example the Menil Collection Museum (Renzo Piano, Houston 1981-1986) and its neighbour the Cy Twombly Gallery (Renzo Piano, Houston 1995) which, using only two independent volumes, generate a thematic unity for which not only the architect is responsible, but also the collectors and the artist in question. Commissions such as these represent a great incentive and orientation for the work of the architect, who is creating a tailor-made construction for each collection or artist, very different to what used to happen in the past, when architects were presented with commissions of an anonymous type, to produce discreet, neutral spaces capable of housing all types of styles, movements and artistic collections.

In addition, the thematic variety of the works on show has made it possible for museums to appear which are not only connected with traditional manifestations of art, but also with other fields of culture and knowledge. The Domus House of Man (Arata Isozaki and César Portela, Corunna 1995), the Museum of Cave Art (William P. Bruder, Phoenix 1994) and the Ancient Provence Research Institute (Henri E. Ciriani, Arles 1996) reflect both the thematic diversity and the desire of medium-sized cities to promote art and culture, by entering into the museum sphere with projects which are on a controlled scale but are never inferior in quality to those put on in the big cities. Currently, the museum not only recognises and contains art, it also brings prestige to a city, fills its citizens with pride and legitimises public authorities and private institutions of diverse origins, thus turning the museum into an important cultural installation, as well as a political instrument of great power and scope. However, we should not be surprised at the great increase in the upsurge in art museums and galleries and cultural centres all over the planet, which, like an architectural typology associated with certain specific guidelines for social behaviour, come onto the market as the international cultural stock exchange rises, to become a highly profitable investment.

The final consequence of the proliferation of, and change in the contemporary exhibition space described above is the enrichment of the museum as an architectural form, a social institution and a public leisure area for citizens and tourists in the industrialised West. The typology and scale of the contemporary museum are as varied as each specific commission.

In the big cities it is common for extensions to be built onto old, prestigious museums, resulting from a need for extra space both for exhibiting new acquisitions and, increasingly, for showing restored art works. This has become common practice in many museums, for example MOMA (Philip L. Goodwin and Edward Durrell Stone, New York 1939), which in 1951 received the addition of the Grace Rainey Rogers Memorial Annex (Philip Johnson and Landes Gores), then in 1964 the East and Garden Wings (Philip Johnson Associates) and finally, in 1984, the Tower Wing Museum (César Pelli & Associates). This type of intervention makes such buildings into extensive cultural infrastructures where it is impossible to see everything in one day; the visitor has to come back a second time or choose a specific section of the museum to visit. The Louvre Museum Pyramid (I. M. Pei, Paris 1987) and the enlargement of the Prado Museum (Rafael Monei, Madrid, 1996-2000) are specific contemporary examples of this custom.

Another of the trends in metropolitan museum-based production is that of the renovation of preexisting spaces or buildings, which on one hand demonstrates a certain respect for the existing architectural heritage, and on the other expresses a desire to exploit a preconsolidated collective memory. The first great project of this type was without doubt Orsay Museum (Act-Architecture and Gae Aulenti, Paris 1986). On this occasion, the magnificent train station designed in 1900 by Victor Laloux was subjected to an intervention which preserved the large central space of the building, while arranging a succession of ascending terraces around it in which the art works are exhibited. The Palace of Fine Art (Jean Marc Ibos and Myrto Vitart, Lille 1990-1992) and the Museum of Contemporary Art (Kleihuhes + Kleihuhes, Berlin 1995) are good examples of renovation which avoided any kind of nostalgic or historicist approach to the original buildings.

Finally there is the new building, designed to revitalise urban centres (Modern Art Museum, Mario Botta, San Francisco, 1991-1995), or to create new poles of attraction at the urban periphery (J. Paul Getty Centre, Richard Meier & Partners, Los Angeles 1997). This kind of museum does not only rejuvenate the urban landscape of the metropolis, but increasingly it also provides medium-sized cities with a cultural infrastructure that had previously only been imagined in the big cities. On a smaller scale (but usually with great stylistic freedom) these projects are surprising both because of their nature and because of the way in which they are inserted into the urban fab-

ric and the landscape. The sobriety of the Galician Contemporary Arts Centre (Álvaro Siza, Santiago de Compostela, 1997), the provocation of the Kunsthal (Rem Koolhaas, Rotterdam 1987-1982) and the magnificent relationship between architecture and landscape represented in the Arken Museum of Modern Art (Soren Robert Lund, Aren 1993) reflect the power that the exhibitory space can achieve on a medium and small scale in non metropolitan areas.

Whatever the strategy used to fulfil a commission to create a museum these days, it is clear that they all have their own personality and identity. Behind all these attitudes that are adopted through the building, it is generally easy to trace positions which may be dogmatic, political or architectural. The ideological role that the cultural and exhibitory space plays nowadays in society is virtually undeniable. All the controversy that arose concerning the project by Frank O. Gehry and Associates for the Bilbao Guggengheim does no more than confirm this fact. The extravagance of the building's forms, its amazing structure and unusual location filled pages and pages of newsprint and minutes of television during the course of 1997, dealing with subjects which ranged from ambitious plans for urban renovation to political power games in the Basque government.

When a museum and its contents are conceived as a whole, as was the case with the Bilbao Guggengheim, such a close complicity between constructed work and exhibited work is created that it seems that are no citizens with half-way opinions on this phenomenon, one which began in the first half of the 20th century with Philip L. Goodwin's and Edward Durrell Stone's MOMA and Frank Lloyd Wright's Guggenheim. The modern paradigm of the museum changed the traditional nineteenth-century concept of the building, by the end of the twentieth century, into a provocative space for showing art. It is obvious that the museum has evolved together with the art it contains and, just like those art works, it has reached a point in which its greatest wealth is based not on its specific material presence, but on questioning what should be the most appropriate stance for it to take.

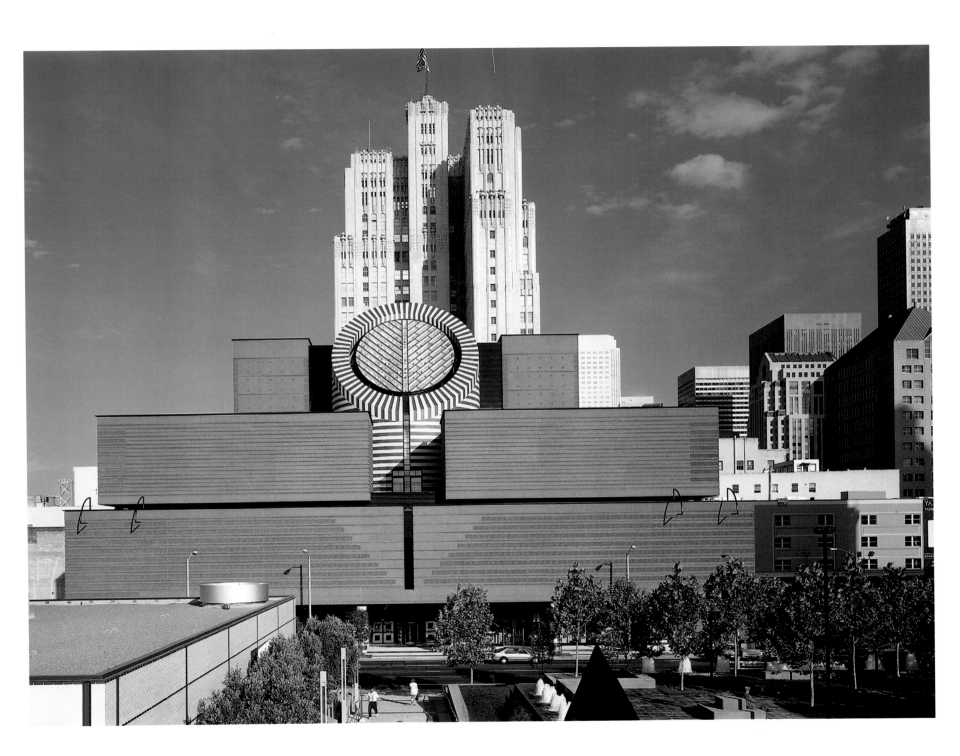